M000103517

THE COLD WAR
(COLOR AND LEARN)

An Illustrated History Coloring Book for Everyone!

Color & Learn

If you like the book, please leave a review on wherever you bought and share your beautiful colored designs with the world.

ISBN-13: 978-1-64845-049-5

Copyright © 2020 by Color & Learn

ALL RIGHTS RESERVED

No part of this book may be reproduced, stored in a retrieval system, or transmitted in any form or by any means, electronic, mechanical, photocopying, recording, scanning, or otherwise, without the prior written permission of the publisher.

GET OUR NEW BOOKS!

Sign up to our VIP Newsletter to not miss our new book releases and to take part of **free book giveaways** and so much more!

www.ColorAndLearn.com/free

CONTENTS

INTRODUCTION

The Cold War wasn't a war in the normal sense of the word. It was a series of wars, protests, conflicts, and events that took place from after World War II until 1991. After World War II ended, the people of Europe were hoping their lives would return to normal and they could go back to working jobs and raising families. With the fascist regimes toppled, most believed there was no reason why they couldn't. But most people never considered that a new, worldwide political battle would replace the one they had just endured.

Joseph Stalin and the Red Army blazed across half of Europe, making sure that most of the governments of Eastern Europe adopted communist governments in the process. American President Harry Truman opposed Stalin and his efforts to spread the ideology of communism, thus setting the stage for more than forty-five years of Cold War battles, from 1945 to 1991.

The stakes of this war were extremely high. Both sides wanted to push their ideas into as many countries as possible and at times were willing to go to war if necessary. But a direct war between the USSR and the USA would have meant World War III, which would have highly likely been the end of civilization as we know it.

The Cold War finally ended with a whimper more than a bang, but its repercussions can still be felt today. Many people involved in the numerous battles and conflicts during the Cold War are still alive and some of the major issues that led to the conflict remain unresolved.

Read ahead and learn about the longest and most important war of the 20th century. You'll be sure to learn a lot about Cold War history and have fun doing it. There are plenty of excellent and exciting illustrations to color, which will bring the Cold War to life wherever you are!

THE EAGLE AND THE BEAR

Unlike most conventional wars in world history, the Cold War didn't begin with a single event or *"shot."* There was no assassination that set it off like in World War I or a massive invasion like what began World War II. No, the Cold War was the result of something that had been simmering for a long time. Not only was this war a struggle between two great nations that never fought each other directly, it was also a war of ideas.

On one side, the United States represented democratic political systems and free enterprise or *capitalist* economies. The symbol of the United States of America is the bald eagle. Americans have historically believed that the bald eagle embodies their ideas of political and economic freedom.

On the other side was the United Soviet Socialist Republics (USSR), more commonly called the Soviet Union. The Soviet Union believed in *communism*, which was a system where the government owned all land, factories, and pretty much everything else. The Soviet Union also only allowed one political party—the Communist Party. Communism came to Russia through a revolution in 1917 and once the communists were in power, they took over their smaller neighboring countries to create the Soviet Union. *"Soviet"* is a Russian word meaning *"council."*

The Soviet Union's symbol was the bear. The people of the Soviet Union believed that the bear represented their country's strength and resilience.

As soon as the shooting of World War II was done, it became clear that *Joseph Stalin*, the dictator of the Soviet Union, wanted to push communism into the countries of Eastern Europe. Once they had pushed the retreating Germans west during World War II, the Soviet Union's *Red Army* quickly occupied most of the countries of Eastern Europe. The Red Army was massive, and the war-weary people of Eastern Europe could do little to stop it, even if they wanted to. Stalin made it clear to American President *Harry Truman* that he was not willing to negotiate his army's occupation of Eastern Europe.

Truman was vehemently opposed to communism because he believed that it was against the American ideals of democracy, free enterprise, and Christianity. In contrast, Stalin was a true blue, or we should say *"red,"* communist who thought that the Soviet Union should use its military to push communism throughout the world.

Before long, both countries began staking out their territory by making alliances and supporting rulers and governments in smaller countries that supported their ideologies. The scene was set for the Cold War.

AN IRON CURTAIN DESCENDS OVER EUROPE

When the Red Army occupied Eastern Europe, Stalin quickly ordered his most trusted people to locate all the pre-World War II communist officials still alive in those countries. The Nazis had managed to kill many, while others had fled in exile, but there were still enough left to ensure that communist, pro-Soviet governments could be installed throughout Eastern Europe.

Stalin supported rigged elections in Eastern Europe to bring communist governments to power, and when that didn't work, he had secret agents start **coup d'états**. A coup d'état usually just called a *"coup,"* is when a government is overthrown by a small group from within.

Within five years after the end of World War II, Poland, Hungary, Romania, Bulgaria, and Czechoslovakia had all become communist and were firmly under the influence of Stalin and the Soviet Union. Yugoslavia and Albania had also become communist, although they weren't as heavily influenced by the Soviets.

The situation worried many in the West. The leaders of the United States, Britain, France, and other Western countries were frustrated and worried that by siding with the Soviet Union against Nazi Germany they had helped make a new enemy, one that was even more powerful. But, as potentially harmful that this new threat was, most leaders were having a difficult time understanding it. Few people in the United States or Western Europe knew much about communism and, after all, the USSR had been the West's ally in World War II.

But former British Prime Minister Winston Churchill knew and understood the threat that communist expansion posed to the West.

On March 5, 1946, Churchill gave a speech at Westminster College in Fulton, Missouri, where he warned about the advance of communism. He declared that *"An iron curtain has descended across the Continent"* and that the Soviet Union was the next major threat to freedom. Since World War II had just concluded and the Soviet Union was an ally of the United States and Britain during the war, most people in those countries didn't think much of the speech for a couple of years.

But as the Soviets became more aggressive in Europe, and as more and more countries became communist, people began to agree with Churchill that Eastern and Western Europe were divided by what seemed like a curtain. It wasn't a real or physical curtain, but it was a political curtain and for those caught behind it in Eastern Europe, it may as well have been made of iron.

THE TERM IS COINED

So now that you know the two major countries involved in the Cold War and some of the reasons why they were at odds, you are probably wondering how and where the term got its name. Well, it is believed that an American businessman named Bernard Baruch (1870–1965) first coined the term when he addressed the South Carolina House of Representatives on April 16, 1947. Baruch had counseled several American presidents before that speech and was familiar with 20th century *geopolitics*. Geopolitics is the word for how countries interact and deal with each other. In his speech, Baruch said:

"Let us not be deceived; we are today in the midst of a Cold War. Our enemies are to be found abroad and at home. Let us never forget this: Our unrest is the heart of their success."

Although Baruch had once been a very influential person, in 1947 many powerful people looked at him as merely a relic of the past. Most people quickly forgot the speech, because like Churchill's *"Iron Curtain Speech,"* many Americans still viewed the Soviet Union as an ally. Still, within two years people throughout the world were referring to the American–Soviet conflict as the Cold War.

But what does the term mean? After all, how can a war be cold?

Yes, wars are very far from being cold. Many people die and there is usually an immense amount of property destruction in any war, especially modern wars. The fact that the United States and the Soviet Union never directly fought each other is what made it *"cold,"* but make no mistakes, they were very much in a war that would influence the world.

Both countries invaded smaller countries at different times during the Cold War and often they would fund and train their smaller allies to fight each other in what are known as *proxy wars*. We'll talk about those later.

The fact that the United States and the Soviet Union never directly fought each other can be attributed more to restraint than anything else. Both sides had military forces that were large enough to overrun most countries and, by the 1960s, they also had nuclear weapons arsenals that could annihilate the world.

The Cold War was a war that both sides wanted to win, but both sides also knew that it was a war that could very easily end everything.

BLOCKADING BERLIN

The Cold War almost turned hot at several points. You'll learn about most of those events in this book, with the first being the *Berlin Blockade* and *Berlin Airlift*. These events began in June 1948, in and around the German city of Berlin. After Germany was defeated, the Soviets occupied the eastern part of Germany, while the Americans, British, and French controlled the western part of Germany.

The city of Berlin was also similarly divided, but the problem for the Western forces was that Berlin was in the middle of the country that would later become East Germany. It was basically a democratic–capitalist island in the middle of communism, behind the Iron Curtain.

West Berlin was supplied, via railroads and highways, by what would become the nation of West Germany. However, on June 24, 1948, Stalin decided to put an end to these activities.

You see, Stalin wanted to make all of Berlin communist. In fact, he wanted to make all of Germany communist, but he knew it wouldn't be easy. He believed that by taking a tough stance the Americans and their allies would back down.

When the Western Allies announced that West Berlin would not use the same money as East Germany, Stalin had the Red Army cut off all rail lines and highways in and out of Berlin. The Soviets also cut off West Berlin's electricity.

With only about a month's worth of supplies, the people of West Berlin faced a potential tragedy. It appears the Western Allies had only two options: retreat or fight.

But then American Army General *Lucius Clay* came up with an idea—fly supplies nonstop from West Germany into West Berlin's Templehof Airport. The Allies used both military and civilian planes to bring food, clothing, oil, and coal to the people of West Berlin starting on June 26, in what became known as the *Berlin Airlift*. The pilots also made sure to bring chocolate and other candy for the children of West Berlin!

The United States Air Force (USAF) and the British Royal Air Force (RAF) flew in the vast majority of the supplies, with a combined 2,326,406 tons of supplies on nearly 280,000 flights. French, Canadian, Australian, New Zealand, and South African pilots also flew supply missions. Since the flights took place day and night, they could be dangerous. 39 British and 31 American servicemen lost their lives, along with 15 German civilians.

After 323 days, on May 12, 1949, Stalin finally backed down by opening the land routes to West Berlin. The Americans had won the first battle of the Cold War, but many more were still to come.

CHINA TURNS RED

On October 1, 1949, a new player entered the Cold War when Mao Zedong (1893–1976) proclaimed that China was a communist country. Many Americans and people throughout the West were shocked that such a large country was now communist. Since China was so populous, it meant that one-quarter of the world's population was then living under a communist government. People everywhere were asking: How did this happen? How did China become red?

Well, it didn't happen overnight, and the United States government was aware of who Mao Zedong was and what he represented. It had all begun during the *Chinese Civil War* (1927–1949), which was between Chinese nationalist forces led by Chiang Kai-shek and Mao Zedong's communists. The two sides actually quit fighting each other and allied against the Japanese during World War II, but once that war was over, they went back at it. The war was tough and very brutal at times, but the communists were successful under Mao's leadership. Mao knew how to motivate his troops and how to effectively use *guerilla warfare*. Guerilla warfare is a war that involves the use of non-conventional types of warfare, including snipers, sabotage, and fighting behind your enemy's front lines.

You're probably wondering, what does the color red have to do with China turning communist? Well, red has traditionally been the color of communism, with communist parties and countries around the world flying different variations of red flags.

China becoming communist proved to be a difficult situation for the Americans. They were totally against the spread of communism, but China was quite different from the Soviet Union. Since it was basically a rural country, it was technologically behind the Soviet Union, so its army didn't appear to pose a threat. China also didn't have nuclear weapons.

Still, many anti-communists in the United States believed that the first strike on China was needed. In the end, President *Harry Truman* decided to take a *"wait and see"* approach to communist China.

It turned out that he didn't have to wait very long.

NATO AND THE WARSAW PACT

Although the Berlin Airlift may have been a victory for the United States, it was clear to President Truman and the American military high command that there would be more political, and possibly military, confrontations with the Soviet Union. The Americans began preparing for a war with the Soviet Union, believing that Europe may well be the location if the Cold War suddenly went hot and turned into World War III.

The leaders of Western Europe also knew that they were vulnerable to the Soviet Union. The Red Army was numerically superior to all the armies of Western Europe combined, so the leaders of the United Kingdom (Great Britain), France, Belgium, the Netherlands, and Luxembourg signed a treaty of alliance in 1948. They were then joined by the United States, Canada, Portugal, Norway, Italy, Denmark, and Iceland on April 4, 1949, to create the *North Atlantic Treaty Organization* or *NATO*. The purpose of NATO was basically to prevent the Soviets from taking any more land in Europe.

Stalin looked at NATO with suspicion but did nothing. At that point, he was becoming an extremely paranoid leader and was more interested in spying, arresting, and executing his own people than he was in spreading communism in Europe.

Stalin's health had been deteriorating and he died in 1953. This caused a brief pause in the Cold War, as many in the West thought that the new Soviet leader, *Nikita Khrushchev*, was more rational. Well, Khrushchev may have been more rational than Stalin, but he was still a diehard communist and a patriot of the Soviet Union. When West Germany joined NATO in 1955, Khrushchev and the Soviet military high command decided to form their own alliance.

On May 14, 1955, the leaders of the communist countries of Poland, Hungary, Czechoslovakia, Bulgaria, Albania, Romania, East Germany, and the Soviet Union met in Warsaw, Poland to form their own military alliance. The alliance was officially known as the **Treaty of Friendship, Cooperation and Mutual Assistance**, but since that was such a mouthful it was often just called the *Warsaw Pact*.

Albania formally withdrew from the Warsaw Pact in 1968. France pulled its troops out of NATO's integrated military command structure in 1966, although it continued to work with the Western powers.

By the late 1950s, the two alliances had massed their forces on either side of the Iron Curtain, with East and West Germany supporting a large share of the bases for both alliances.

NATO

WARSAW PACT

DID YOU KNOW?

- As you can probably already tell, the Soviet Union liked to give its organizations long names. Its army was officially known as the *"Workers' and Peasants' Red Army,"* but that was usually just abbreviated to the *"Red Army."* The Red Army officially changed its name in 1946 to the *"Soviet Army,"* but many in the West continued to call it the *"Red Army."*

- During the Cold War, the term *"West"* generally referred to the U.S., its NATO allies in Western Europe, and their other allies throughout the world. It wasn't necessarily a cultural designation, though. Countries in Asia that were aligned with the U.S., such as the Philippines and Japan, were often referred to as part of the West during the Cold War.

- After losing the Chinese Civil War, Chiang Kei-shek and the nationalists retreated to the island of Formosa/Taiwan, where they established their own government.

- NATO was formed just before the Berlin Airlift ended. Some historians believe that the formation of NATO was another signal to Stalin that the West wouldn't back down.

- The USSR tested its first atomic bomb on August 29, 1949.

- France left NATO largely due to its historical rivalry with Britain. French President Charles de Gaulle thought that the U.S. and Britain were too close and leaving France out of many of the important decisions.

- The United Kingdom/Britain tested its first atomic bomb on October 3, 1952.

- West Germany was officially known as the Federal Republic of Germany. Its capital was in the city of Bonn. East Germany was officially the German Democratic Republic with its capital in East Berlin. They officially became separate countries in 1949.

TRUMAN'S DOCTRINE

America's policies during the early Cold War were largely the result of President Truman's ideas. Truman was President Roosevelt's vice president for most of World War II, but he often disagreed with his boss about Stalin and the Soviet Union. Roosevelt viewed the Soviet Union as a true ally, while Truman believed that in many ways, the USSR posed just as much of a threat as Nazi Germany did. When Truman became president in 1945, he was able to pursue his anti-communist ideas more fully.

Truman vowed to the U.S. Congress on March 12, 1947, that he would do everything in his power to stop the spread of communism. He said he would support anti-communist governments, or those fighting communist governments, through a variety of means. Part of his speech stated:

"I believe it must be the policy of the United States to support free peoples who are resisting attempted subjugation by armed minorities or by outside pressures."

Truman then followed this up by giving U.S. economic support to the Greek government in its war against communist guerillas during the **Greek Civil War** (1946–1949). The anti-communist forces were successful in that war, which was seen by many as a victory for Truman's anti-communist ideas. Truman's plan to confront the spread of communism by a variety of means became known as the **Truman Doctrine.** A doctrine is an idea or belief, so in this case it refers to anti-communism. The Truman Doctrine was carried out by Truman and pretty much every American president after him until 1991.

The Truman Doctrine led to the U.S. getting directly involved in some armed conflicts (as we'll see in a bit) and at other times supporting proxies (we'll also talk about that a bit later). It also meant that sometimes the Americans were willing to support corrupt dictators, as long as they were anti-communist!

The Soviets, and later the Chinese, viewed the Truman Doctrine as an attempt by the Americans to control the world. They called it an example of *"Yankee imperialism"* and thought it was something that should be confronted.

By the early 1950s it was clear that neither side was backing down.

THE KOREAN WAR

When World War II ended, Germany was not the only country that was forcibly divided. As Japan's short-lived Asian empire collapsed, the Red Army occupied the northern part of the Korean Peninsula. In 1948, Korea was officially divided, with the northern part becoming the **Democratic People's Republic of Korea**, or North Korea. The southern part of Korea became the Republic of Korea, or South Korea. Almost from the beginning, North Korea wanted to control the democratic–capitalist South Korea and threatened it on several occasions.

Then, on June 25, 1950, North Korean forces invaded South Korea, starting the **Korean War**. The North Koreans prepared ahead of time for the war and were better armed and trained than their South Korean counterparts. The North Koreans had arms from the Soviet Union and used those, along with their surprise attack, to push the South Koreans south on the peninsula.

The **United Nations** condemned North Korea's attack and President Truman immediately ordered American troops to Korea. The British, and many of their former colonies, also sent thousands of troops to fight the North Koreans.

By September, the situation looked bleak. The North Koreans had pushed the South Koreans, Americans, and United Nations allies to the southern tip of Korea, which became known as the **Pusan Perimeter**. After holding their ground, the allies then did a major counterattack from September 10, 1950, which became known as the **Battle of Ichon**.

The course of the war rapidly changed in the following months. The Americans and their allies steadily pushed north, closer to China.

China sent its massive army into the war in November and first met the Americans in a major engagement at the **Battle of Chosin Reservoir**, from November 27 to December 13, 1950. Although the Americans killed far more Chinese soldiers in the battle, they lost more than 1,000 men and were forced to slowly retreat.

The Chinese kept sending wave after wave of soldiers towards the Americans. Many of the Chinese didn't even have guns! They would attack with shovels and pick up guns lying on the ground. By early 1951, the massive numbers of Chinese were able to drive the Americans and their allies back to the original line dividing North and South Korea—the **38th Parallel**.

Fighting in Korea continued until an **armistice** was signed on July 27, 1953. An armistice is basically an agreement to stop fighting, but it is not quite a formal peace treaty. The two sides agreed to go back to the original line that divided North and South Korea, the 38th Parallel. More than 500,000 soldiers on both sides were killed or wounded in the war, including nearly 37,000 Americans killed.

REAL LIFE SPY GAMES

Many of the Cold War battles were played out in secret by spies who routinely changed sides for several reasons. The primary spy agency for the Soviet Union was the KGB (we'll get to them in the next section) and for the United States it was the Central Intelligence Agency (CIA). Most experts today agree that the Soviet Union's army of spies was far larger and better organized than the Americans.

The Soviets knew that the Americans and their allies were ahead of them technologically and that no amount of money they spent would help them catch up, so they caught up to them the old-fashioned way—by stealing information from them!

The Soviets made their first major spy move by stealing American atomic weapons secrets. They used a variety of methods and approaches to entice American scientists working on the *Manhattan Project*, which was the program to build the first atomic bombs.

Greed was a common appeal used by Soviet secret agents. They simply offered American scientists nice sums of money to turn over secrets. At other times, the agents would *blackmail* Americans. Blackmail is when a person has damaging information on someone, usually personal, that they use to get that person to do something for them. Finally, some Soviet agents would use ideology or common background to *"turn"* American scientists. Many of the Jewish scientists working on the Manhattan project had family members from Russia or were from Russia themselves. Others saw communism in a sympathetic light, because the communists had stood up to the fascists during World War II.

Julius and Ethel Rosenberg fell into the last category.

Although both Julius and his wife Ethel were born in the United States, their families were Jewish immigrants from Russia. Julius was also a former member of the Communist Party USA. Julius was kicked out of the Army during World War II for his membership in the Communist Party in 1944. Before he was drummed out of the army, Rosenberg was able to recruit a few men working on the Manhattan Project for a Soviet spy ring.

Along with his wife Ethel, Julius worked as a middleman, funneling information from spies working on the Manhattan Project to Soviet agents. The Rosenbergs were successful at getting the information to the Soviets, who were able to build their first atomic bomb in 1949, referred to by the Americans as *Joe-1* for Joseph Stalin.

The Rosenbergs were caught in 1950, arrested for *espionage* (spying), convicted, and sentenced to death. They were both executed in 1953.

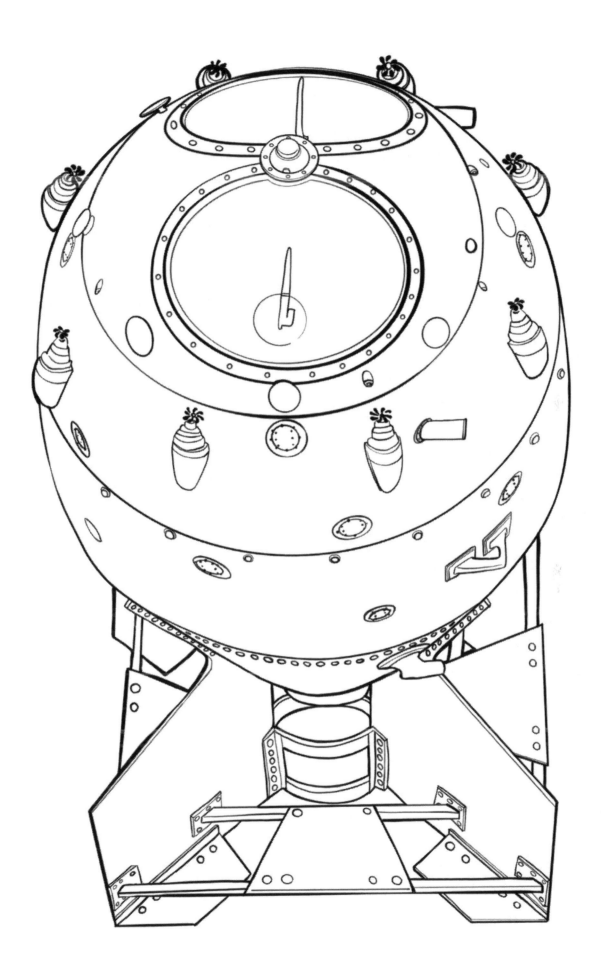

KGB

The Soviet Union's premier spy, or *"intelligence"* agency, was the **Committee for State Security**, which was usually abbreviated as *"KGB."* If you're wondering how they got KGB from the actual name of the agency, remember that the official language of the Soviet Union was Russian, and that the Russian language uses a different form of writing known as *Cyrillic*.

What is important to know, is that the KGB officially formed in 1954, out of earlier Soviet spy agencies. Once it formed, it didn't take long for the KGB to become the most effective intelligence agency in the world.

The KGB successfully *turned* hundreds of agents and civilians around the world, giving the Soviets valuable information about American, British, and other allies' military, economic, and perhaps most importantly, scientific research.

The KGB used all the tricks of the espionage trade, known as *tradecraft*. Some of these methods and devices included using dead drops, employing sophisticated encryption devices, elaborate concealment structures, and even some weapons that would make James Bond proud!

The KGB had its greatest success sending its own spies onto American soil. Some of the Soviet spies in America had legitimate diplomatic visas, but many were in the country under false identities. These spies became known as *illegals*.

The illegals learned English and American customs and developed elaborate backstories of their fake lives that were known as *legends*. Once the spy had mastered the English language and American customs, the KGB would smuggle him into the United States where he would hopefully find employment in an important company or government agency.

The American CIA began successfully countering the illegal agents by the late 1950s, so the KGB shifted their focus. They began approaching Americans directly through blackmail, having sympathy to their cause, or with large sums of money.

The KGB continued to play an important role throughout the Cold War. Wherever the Americans were doing something big, you could be sure there were KGB agents nearby, reporting their findings back to Moscow.

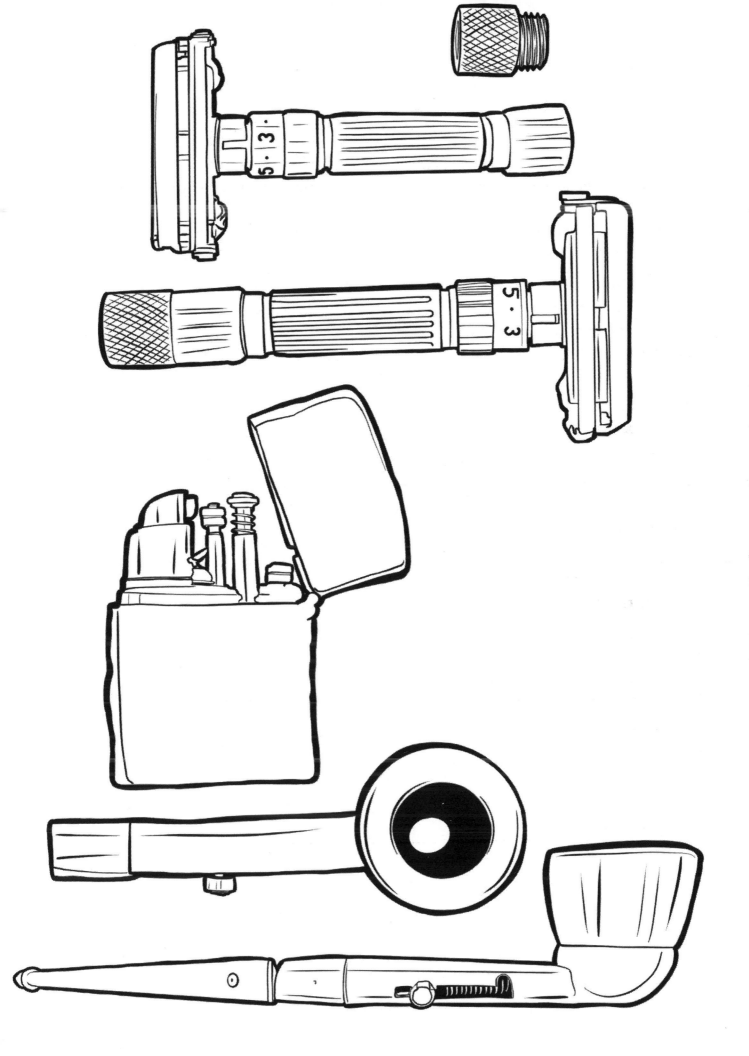

THE RED SCARE

Back in the 1950s the United States was a different place. Things were slower, crime was much lower, and technology was less advanced. It was an era when World War II veterans were starting families and the *"Baby Boom"* was beginning. It was also the beginning of the Cold War.

Americans loved what they had and didn't want to lose it, so they began to view the Soviet Union and the threat of communism in a different way. Communism in general became the enemy to most Americans, and there was a real fear that at any moment either the Soviets would attack with their army and nuclear weapons, or communists would somehow take over the American government. This fear of communism in the 1950s became known as the *Red Scare*. Remember, red was the color of communism.

At the front of the war against communism in the United States was Wisconsin Senator *Joseph McCarthy* (1908–1957). McCarthy not only warned of the threat of a communist takeover by the Soviets, but also claimed that he had lists of communists, communist sympathizers, and Soviet spies in the American government. Many hearings were conducted by Congress to check McCarthy's claims and he was a popular political figure for a while. McCarthy was so powerful that the term *McCarthyism* was named for him. McCarthyism refers to the sometimes-extreme methods some people used to find communists. Although there did turn out to be some communists in the government, McCarthy made many enemies during his crusade and eventually lost favor.

Another part of the Red Scare was the *House Un-American Activities Committee (HUAC)*. This was a committee formed within the U.S. House of Representatives in 1938 to investigate communist activities in the United States. Many former Soviet spies were called to testify, including accused spy *Alger Hiss*. The HUAC was also known for creating the Hollywood *Blacklist* in the 1950s. The Blacklist was an unofficial list of Hollywood actors, directors, producers, and writers who were believed to be either communists or sympathetic to communism.

Those on the Blacklist often found it nearly impossible to work in the United States until well into the 1970s.

THE HUNGARIAN REVOLUTION

In 1956, most people in the world believed that communism would never end. It was believed that the Iron Curtain was impenetrable and that all the communist countries behind it would never even attempt to break away from the Soviet Union's influence.

This seemed to be the case until protests broke out in Budapest, Hungary on June 23, 1956.

As is the case throughout most of history, college students, who wanted more freedom, led the protests. The students were upset with communism in general and specifically Hungary's repressive government. The protests spread throughout Hungary that summer but didn't turn violent until October 23. On that day, protesters tore down a statue of Joseph Stalin, which led to units of the Hungarian police opening fire.

But the reality is that most of the Hungarian police didn't want to fire on their own people, so they stood down. The Soviet Army then came in to take their place, which is when things got very tense and violent.

The Hungarian government collapsed under the pressure from both the inside and outside, so a new government led by *Imre Nagy* took power. Free elections would be held and most importantly, Hungary would leave the Warsaw Pact. Anti-communist Hungarians began organizing into groups and stockpiling weapons. One of the most common weapons the Hungarian freedom fighters used was the *Molotov cocktail*. A Molotov cocktail is simply a bottle filled with gas or some other type of flammable liquid. The freedom fighters would throw Molotov cocktails at Soviet tanks from their perches on top of buildings.

The Hungarian freedom fighters also used other guerilla tactics against the Soviets, including snipers, sabotage, and hit and run attacks. The tactics seemed to be successful, because the Soviets appeared to be leaving Hungary by early November.

The world was watching on tenterhooks for what would happen next. Was the Soviet Union going to back down?

On November 4, more than 30,000 Soviet soldiers reentered Hungary, with more than 1,000 tanks. The freedom fighters were quickly overwhelmed, and the fighting was finished by November 11. Many of the leaders of the Hungarian Revolution, including Imre Nagy, were arrested and later executed. Over 2,500 Hungarians and 700 Soviet soldiers died in the fighting. More than 200,000 Hungarians had to flee the country, many ending up in the United States.

The Americans and their allies decided not to send aid to the Hungarian rebels.

Nikita Khrushchev and the Soviet Union won the battle in Hungary, but the Cold War was still far from finished.

ANTI-COLONIAL REBELLIONS

The major battlegrounds of the Cold War were usually far from Europe or North America, in countries that were once *colonial possessions* of European powers. Most of these countries were in Africa and the Middle East and were formerly ruled by Britain and France. After World War II, the old colonial powers were troubled with economic problems and were unable to keep hold of all their colonies.

One by one, the colonies began breaking away, sometimes violently, while at other times more or less peacefully.

India broke away from the British Empire in 1947. This was followed by many of Britain's African colonies breaking away in the 1950s, often violently. Throughout what is now the nation of Kenya, native rebels attacked British authorities and citizens in the *Mau Uprising* (1952–1960). Although the British were able to put down the Mau Mau Uprising, it cost them dearly and they were forced to allow the Kenya Colony to become independent. The British were also driven out of Egypt in 1952, Jordan in 1957, and Malaysia also in 1957, among other colonies.

Although the French had fewer colonies, they too were driven out of Africa in the 1950s. The French tried to hold their colony of Algeria during the bloody *Algerian War of Independence* (1854–1962), but like the British in Kenya, found that it was too costly to keep control and so gave the Algerians independence.

All these anti-colonial rebellions had a tremendous impact on the Cold War. Many of the anti-colonial rebels adopted beliefs that were sympathetic to communism (if not directly communist). The Soviet Union attempted to extend its influence in these newly independent countries by supporting communist parties, providing weapons, and sending advisors to support communist guerrillas.

The United States also became heavily involved in many of the former British and French colonies. The Americans sent CIA agents to infiltrate these countries and sometimes also funded armed right-wing guerillas and right-wing governments that were in power.

The battles in these small countries usually didn't change the course of the Cold War much, but sometimes, like in Cuba, the results had some big repercussions.

CASTRO AND CUBA

Although communism was a very real fear for most Americans in the 1950s, it was one that was still far away. Most of the Cold War battles being fought were far from the United States and the government seemed to be doing everything it could to eliminate an internal communist takeover in the United States.

But all of that changed on January 1, 1959.

On that day, *Fidel Castro* and his band of revolutionaries took over the Cuban government. Most Americans didn't know much about Castro at that time. They knew that he liked to smoke cigars, wore military fatigues, and had a beard. They also knew that his brother was named Raul and his right-hand man was an Argentine of Spanish and Irish descent, named *Ernesto "Che" Guevara*. Che also had a beard.

The situation that led Castro to power is important in the Cold War and not very surprising. A guy named *Fulgencio Batista* came to power in 1952 through a military coup. Batista ignored the Cuban people's rights and only served to make himself wealthy by working with the rich, including the American mafia. Mafia is an organized group of criminals.

People began resisting Batista's rule and eventually the Castro brothers and a small group of other rebels attacked a military barracks on July 26, 1953. They hoped to get some arms (weapons and ammunition) and start a revolution, but instead they were arrested and exiled (kicked out and barred) from Cuba. While the Castro brothers were living in Mexico, they met Guevara. Even though Guevara came from a well-to-do family, he was a die-hard communist.

Guevara was also an excellent tactician in guerilla warfare tactics. A tactician is someone who is good at planning strategies.

The Castro brothers and Guevara secretly returned to Cuba in 1956 and promptly started a guerilla warfare campaign in the *Sierra Maestra Mountains*. The revolutionary forces moved into the capital of Santiago in late December 1958 and Batista and his government ministers then fled the country. Castro was smoking cigars in the presidential palace on January 1, 1959!

At first the United States was willing to recognize Castro, but when it became clear that he was going to be a dictator and basically a communist, things changed. Castro *nationalized* all American companies and properties in Cuba. This means that the Cuban government owned those businesses from that point forward. So, the Americans froze all Cuban financial assets in the United States.

In response, Castro took steps to strengthen relations with the Soviet Union.

FALLING DOMINOES

On January 20, 1953, there was a new sheriff in town. Well, there was a new American president, ***Dwight. D. Eisenhower*** (1890–1969). Eisenhower was a well-known and beloved public figure in the United States. He was the Supreme Commander of the Allied forces in World War II, so when he ran as a Republican in the 1952 U.S. Presidential Election, he won by a landslide. He also won re-election by a landslide in 1956.

Eisenhower's presidency was known for peace and prosperity on the home front and a vigorous opposition to the Soviet Union and communism globally. One of the best things Eisenhower was known for was coming up with what is known as the ***"Domino Theory."***

During a press conference on April 7, 1954, Eisenhower described the process by which small countries became communist, like dominoes lined up being knocked over—once you knocked over one, they would all fall.

"You have a row of dominoes set up, you knock over the first one, and what will happen to the last one is the certainty that it will go over very quickly," said Eisenhower.

Eisenhower was particularly talking about Asia and the French colony of ***Indochina***. Indochina was a colony that later became the countries of Vietnam, Cambodia, and Laos. He thought that once China became communist, a domino effect would be created throughout the entire region. One month after Eisenhower gave his Domino Theory speech, the French left Indochina and the communists quickly moved in and took control of North Vietnam. The first American troops entered Vietnam the following year.

The Domino Theory would continue to play a major role in the Cold War in the 1960s, both in Vietnam and then in the 1970s and '80s in Latin America. Successive American presidents believed that if even one country became communist, then more could follow, so they had to do what they could to stop it.

Communists around the world saw the Domino Theory from another side. Che Guevara (remember him?) wrote in 1967 that if there were enough *"Vietnams"* in different regions of the world, then capitalist governments would begin toppling one after another.

By the 1960s dominoes were about to topple all over the world, but it wasn't a game!

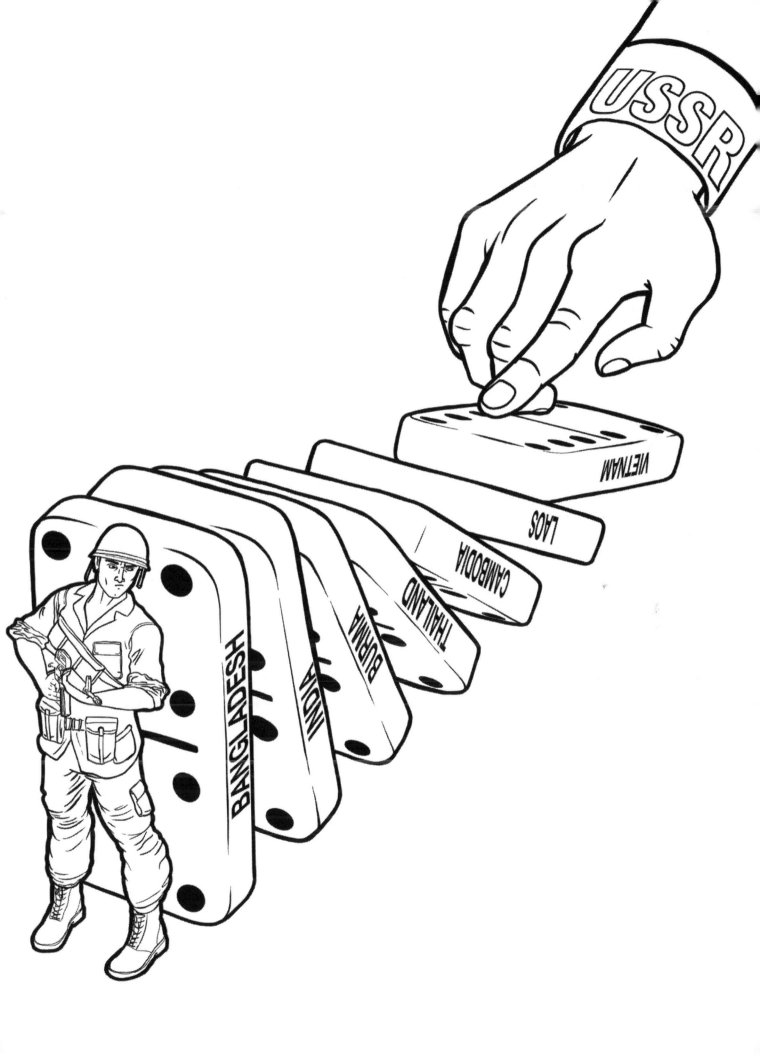

THE U-2 INCIDENT

As we talked about earlier, there was a lot of spying going on during the Cold War. The Soviets were generally better and more successful at the spy game, but the Americans and their allies were also quite good at it. Spying could be a dangerous game: agents could be killed or captured, which could jeopardize a mission. On May 1, 1960, a failed American spy mission almost turned the Cold War hot.

On that day, American pilot Francis Gary Powers was flying a U-2 spy plane over an isolated section of central Russia when he was shot down by a Soviet surface-to-air missile. Powers parachuted to safety, but he was captured and served two years in a Soviet prison.

The shooting down of the U-2 was important because it created new tension between the USA and USSR, who had been slowly moving towards better relations.

The shooting down of the plane also meant that the Soviets gained possession of advanced American technology. And make no mistake about it, the U-2 spy plane was much more advanced than anything the Soviets had in their arsenal.

The U-2 planes could fly at an altitude of up to 70,000 feet, day or night, rain or shine. The U-2's capabilities meant that no Soviet jet could keep up with it, although on May 1 it was demonstrated that U-2s couldn't outrun S-75 Dvina surface-to-air missiles.

The Americans initially tried to *cover up* the incident, but Soviet leader Nikita Khrushchev went public with it in a press conference. The incident proved to be a propaganda victory for the Soviet Union in some ways but was overall a stalemate as a Cold War battle (a stalemate counts as a draw). The Americans continued to fly U-2 missions over the Soviet Union but were more cautious because they knew that the Soviet surface-to-air missiles were capable of taking them down. Powers was released when the Americans *"traded"* him for a Soviet spy.

The biggest impact of the U-2 Spy Plane Incident was that it confirmed that the Cold War was far from over.

FIRST QUIZ TIME!

1. Joseph Stalin was the leader of which country?

    a. USSR/Soviet Union
    b. USA/America
    c. China

2. Which of these countries *did not* become communist?

    a. China
    b. Cuba
    c. UK/Great Britain

3. This was the nickname of the line that divided communist Eastern Europe from Western Europe

    a. Iron Curtain
    b. Iron Chef
    c. Iron Man

4. What was the Warsaw Pact?

    a. A group of Polish food enthusiasts
    b. A military alliance of European communist countries
    c. A group of football/soccer hooligans

5. American troops fought directly against Chinese troops in this war

    a. The Mau Mau Uprising
    b. The Korean War
    c. The Suez Crisis

INTERESTING QUOTES

Ideas are far more powerful than guns.
We don't let our people have guns.
Why should we let them have ideas?

Joseph Stalin

You have enemies? Good.
That means you've stood up for something, sometime in your life.

Winston S. Churchill

We cannot be sure of having something to live for
unless we are willing to die for it.
Che Guevara

KHRUSHCHEV VISITS AMERICA

When Joseph Stalin died in 1953, there was a brief period when it was unknown who would be the next leader of the Soviet Union's Communist Party and the leader of the country. As you know, the torch was passed to Nikita Khrushchev (1894–1971). Within the Soviet Union, Khrushchev pursued a policy of *de-Stalinization*, which meant that he freed many of the people put in prison by Stalin. He also reversed many of Stalin's repressive policies. Khrushchev then embarked on an ambitious campaign to expand the Soviet Union's agricultural production. He called this program the *virgin lands* program, because it was meant to make normally unproductive land into fertile fields. The virgin lands program was only partially successful.

Make no mistake, though, Khrushchev was a true communist who did whatever he could to expand the Soviet Union's influence and to limit the influence of the U.S. in the world. We've already looked at how he did that by forming the Warsaw Pact and putting down the Hungarian Revolution. Those events show us that Khrushchev was a much more modern dictator than Stalin.

Khrushchev wore Western style suits instead of the military garb that Stalin wore, and he seemed to have a better personality. To most Americans, the bald Khrushchev seemed like much more of a normal guy than Stalin.

Khrushchev promoted his public persona further when he visited the United States in September 1959. Not only did he meet with President Eisenhower to discuss the tense situation in Berlin, he also traveled extensively, visiting a movie studio in Hollywood, a supermarket in San Francisco, and a family farm in Iowa.

The Soviet leader also made numerous trips to the United Nations' headquarters in New York, where he railed against American *"imperialism."* Imperialism means when a larger country or government grows stronger by taking over poorer or weaker countries.

Instead of spending most of his country's resources to support communist guerillas around the world, Khrushchev increased the Soviet Union's long-range *intercontinental ballistic missile* arsenal. These missiles could carry a nuclear warhead and travel distances of up to 7,000 miles. The problem Khrushchev faced was Eisenhower. He knew that it would be difficult to push the old war hero around, but in 1960 the American people elected a new president, who was quite young and inexperienced.

Would Khrushchev have his way with him?

"ICH BIN EIN BERLINER"

When Democrat John F. Kennedy (1917–1963) was elected President of the United States, Americans saw him as a youthful symbol of the future. He was handsome, his wife was pretty, and he spoke well, despite a heavy Massachusetts accent.

But Khrushchev saw Kennedy as weak and soft and a president he could probably intimidate.

Not long after Kennedy was inaugurated in January 1961, Khrushchev ordered a major buildup of Warsaw Pact troops around Berlin. Khrushchev, like Stalin before him, wanted the Berlin issue resolved in the Soviet Union's favor. Khrushchev gave the Western powers in West Berlin (the US, UK, and France) an ultimatum in 1958: pull out all your troops and turn control of West Berlin over to East Germany. Doing so would have effectively made West Berlin a part of East Germany and therefore communist. Eisenhower ignored the ultimatum and Khrushchev dropped the issue.

Khrushchev then reissued the ultimatum to President Kennedy on June 4, 1961, when the two leaders met in Vienna, Austria. The Soviet leader believed he could intimidate and/or talk circles around the young American leader. At first it appeared that he was right.

Kennedy publicly agreed that the Soviets had a right to be in the region, but then he stated to the American people that four Army and two Marine divisions would be sent to Europe. The president then gave a speech in West Berlin to the German people where he stated, *"Ich Bin Ein Berliner,"* which is translated as *"I am a Berliner."*

The communist East German government responded to the crisis by beginning construction of the **Berlin Wall** in August 1961. Before that, nearly one million people had escaped the Iron Curtain by passing through the relatively lax West Berlin–East Berlin border, but that was no longer the case. The single access point between the two sectors of the city, known as **Checkpoint Charlie**, became the scene of a tense standoff.

NATO and Warsaw Pact troops were on high alert and things became even more tense when Soviet and American tanks began amassing on either side of Checkpoint Charlie in late October. The whole world was watching the nightly news, waiting to see if this was where the next world war would start. Some of the tanks were within mere feet of each other! Finally, on October 28, both sides ordered their tanks to stand down.

The world had avoided another close call, but there would be many more to come.

TWELVE DAYS THE WORLD STOOD STILL

As important as the Berlin Crisis was, it was round two in the Kennedy–Khrushchev conflict. Since everything stayed virtually the same after the Berlin Crisis, let's say that that round was a draw (or a stalemate!). But rounds one and three took place in Cuba.

Round one happened when President Kennedy gave the go ahead for a CIA sponsored *covert* invasion of Cuba on April 17, 1961. Cuban dissidents and exiles, who were trained by the CIA and US military, attempted to invade Cuba on a coastline known as the ***Bay of Pigs***. The invasion, which became known as the ***Bay of Pigs Invasion***, was brutally put down by the Cuban Army by April 20. There was no doubt that it was a victory for Castro, Khrushchev, and world communism.

By late 1962, the score was: Khrushchev 1 and one draw.

The third and final round of the conflict took place from October 16 to October 28, 1962, in what is now known as the ***Cuban Missile Crisis***.

It all began when the United States began putting nuclear missiles in the country of Turkey. From Turkey, the United States would be able to strike any major target in the USSR or its Warsaw Pact allies. It was surely a major threat, and when combined with what had just transpired in Berlin, Khrushchev felt pressure to meet the perceived American threat. After the attempted Bay of Pigs invasion, Khrushchev saw his chance.

The Soviet leader promised generous aid for Cuba if they agreed to allow the USSR to install nuclear missile bases. The construction of missile silos began, but in early October 1962 American U-2 spy planes (remember them?) took photos of the silos being constructed in Cuba.

Kennedy immediately met with the military high command to plan a strategy. He decided that the US Navy would blockade the island of Cuba—no ships could enter or leave the island. The president spoke to the nation on October 22, in honest yet stark terms. He gave Khrushchev and Castro an ultimatum: if the nuclear sites weren't removed from Cuba, the US would invade the island with the full force of its military.

The world waited breathlessly for anything to happen. An itchy trigger-finger on either side could have very easily started World War III. But in the end, cooler heads prevailed. The Cuban Missile Crisis ended on October 28 when Khrushchev agreed to dismantle the nuclear sites in Cuba. In return, Kennedy agreed to dismantle American nuclear sites in Turkey and Italy. The two countries also agreed to establish a *"hotline,"* which was a red colored phone that connected the leaders of both countries directly.

FALLOUT SHELTERS WERE BIG BUSINESS

As both sides continued to build their nuclear weapon arsenals, it was clear to everyone that if World War III were to happen, it would probably involve a lot of nuclear weapons that could fall on cities all over the world. After the atomic bombs were dropped on Hiroshima and Nagasaki, the world saw the devastation that a nuclear bomb could cause. Those bombs not only destroyed all buildings and life near the impact points, but they also unleashed deadly radiation that continued to kill people for years in the form of cancer and other ailments. But by the early 1960s, nuclear weapons were much more powerful, accurate, and could be launched from multiple locations.

Leaders on both sides began building extensive underground *bunker* networks where they could continue their governments, even if everything was virtually destroyed on the surface.

After the Cuban Missile Crisis, Americans saw just how vulnerable they were. Who would have thought that this was good news for some!

The United States is the center of the capitalist universe, which means that there is always someone looking to cash in on new ideas. And sometimes people are looking to cash in on misfortune.

Under President Kennedy, the government began building community *fallout shelters* across the United States. Fallout shelters were made of concrete and often built partially underground to protect people from a nuclear blast and the harmful radiation, or *fallout*, that would fall to the earth afterward. Fallout shelters were stocked with food and other provisions.

But some people just wouldn't feel safe sharing a fallout shelter with strangers. They also needed to get to their shelter as soon as possible. So, if you had enough money in the early 1960s, you could contact any number of companies that specialized in building fallout shelters in people's backyards! Or if you were a little short on cash, you could build a fallout shelter in your basement.

Between 1961, just after the Cuban Missile Crisis, and 1963, there was a major boom in home fallout shelter construction in the United States. Companies formed, offering their services in magazines, usually for a hefty price. Home fallout shelters were often cozy and well-stocked with plenty of food, water, and other provisions. The problem was that when nuclear war didn't happen the market bottomed out. There was a slight resurgence of home fallout shelter construction in the 1980s when nuclear war fears happened again, but it was nothing compared to the early 1960s.

If you look around backyards in America today you might even find an old fallout shelter!

THE SPACE RACE

The Cold War was truly a war that took place on pretty much every continent on earth. By the late 1950s, the Cold War was even taken into outer space in what became known as the *Space Race*. It was believed that whichever side controlled space would also be able to win the Cold War. After all, if your side figured out how to put nuclear missiles into space then you had quite an advantage, right?

The Space Race really began during World War II. The Soviet Union had been experimenting with rocket technology, but Germany was far ahead of them. After the war, the Soviets were able to take much of the Germans' rocket technology back to Moscow, while the Americans took many of the German rocket scientists, such as *Wernher von Braun*, back to the United States.

The first victory in the Space Race went to the Soviet Union. On October 4, 1957, the Soviets launched *Sputnik I*, the first artificial satellite. A satellite is an object that revolves around a planet, like our moon, but the Sputnik was the first satellite made by people. The event frightened and alarmed Americans. Just one month later, on November 3, the Soviets sent the first living animal into space. The animal was a female dog named *Laika* and although she probably died not long after entering space, she became a hero in the USSR.

President Eisenhower had to react. Eisenhower signed an act into law that made the *National Aeronautics and Space Administration (NASA)* the American government agency that would lead the Space Race.

But before the Americans could do anything, the Soviets made space history once more when *Yuri Gargarin* became the first human in space on April 12, 1961.

The situation was becoming scarier and scarier for the Americans, so when Kennedy became president, he made it his top priority to win the Space Race. The plan was to put a man on the moon before the Soviets. To do this, the Americans created the *Apollo Program*, which was a series of space missions with the goal of landing on the moon. The goal was finally realized on July 20, 1969, when American astronaut Neil Armstrong became the first human to set foot on the moon during the Apollo 11 mission.

In many ways, the Space Race helped to bring peace more than anything else. During the 1970s, American astronauts and Soviet *cosmonauts* (the Russian word for astronaut) worked together on the *Apollo-Soyuz Project*. The knowledge gained from space exploration was then used more for peaceful purposes.

DID YOU KNOW?

- Despite some pretty high tensions at times between the USA and USSR, neither country ever closed its embassy in the other country. Embassy employees were sometimes expelled and deported if they were caught red-handed doing espionage, but the embassies themselves were never closed. Basically, closing an embassy would look bad to the rest of the world and it also would have blown good cover for spying!

- Modern historians and political scientists often classify political ideas on a scale that goes from left to right. Communism is generally considered on the leftwing of the scale, while capitalism is on the rightwing.

- The original organization that led the Cuban Revolution was called the Movimiento 26 de Julio, or the *26ᵗʰ of July Movement* in English. After Castro achieved victory, the 26ᵗʰ of July Movement became part of the United Party of the Socialist Revolution of Cuba, which was the only legal political party in the country.

- Many communist governments and parties throughout history referred to themselves as *"socialist,"* although non-communists have also used that label. Political scientists generally consider socialists to be to the left of the center of the political spectrum, while communists are to the left of socialists.

- You're probably wondering why USSR was spelled CCCP on Soviet equipment and uniforms? The reason is because the Russian language, and many other eastern European languages, use the *Cyrillic* alphabet in their writing. The Cyrillic alphabet was based on the Greek alphabet, so it looks a little different than the writing of most Western European languages, such as English, which are based on the Latin alphabet.

- The term *bloc* was commonly used during the Cold War. It is just another name for an alliance or grouping of nations. The Western Bloc usually referred to the US and its allies, including NATO. The Eastern or Communist Bloc was a reference to the USSR and its allies.

COLD WAR CINEMA

Although the Cold War was a scary event, it wasn't all bad. There were a bunch of movies made in the West, mainly the United States, which dealt with Cold War themes and events. Some of these movies and television shows used humor to look at the situation, while others presented a picture of a terrifying future if the Cold War were ever to turn hot. Other movies used hidden messages to hide what the writers and directors really thought about current events.

Nearly every film and television show made during and about the Cold War portrayed it as a bad situation, but they did differ in their details. *The Day After* was a 1983 film that portrayed the effects of nuclear war in and around Kansas City, Missouri. The movie focused on the devastation the war caused and showed that no one was really a winner. Similarly, many episodes of the 1950s–1960s television show, *The Twilight Zone*, also explored the idea of the Cold War turning hot. In most of those episodes, World War III was depicted as a war that no side really won and that survivors had to learn from the mistakes of their leaders.

The 1984 movie *Red Dawn* approached the Cold War and World War III from another angle. Instead of focusing on nuclear war, the plot of *Red Dawn* involved the Russians and Cubans invading America. The heroes of this film were American teenagers who banded together to wage a guerilla campaign against the communist occupiers.

Several American and British films depicted espionage and spying, the most famous of which were the *James Bond* films. Espionage themed television shows such as *Mission Impossible*, *The Man from U.N.C.L.E.*, and *Danger Man* were all extremely popular in America and Britain during the 1960s.

There were also some movies that tackled Cold War themes in more subtle ways. The 1956 film *Invasion of the Body Snatchers* was seen by many as both anti-communist and anti-Red Scare, but director Don Siegel stated that the movie never had a true political statement. Likewise, *The Manchurian Candidate* (1962) was a movie about a communist takeover of America, but it was equally critical of Red Scare paranoia.

All these films and television shows influenced opinions in the West about the Soviet Union and the Cold War. Today they are still important pieces of Cold War and film history.

WHAT WERE PROXY WARS?

We've already used the term *proxy war* a few times in our study of the Cold War, so you probably have a fairly good idea of what it is. But let's investigate the term a little more and look at some important examples during the Cold War.

A proxy is someone or something who is given power or authority to act on behalf of another person or thing. When it comes to wars and nations, it is simply a country that is fighting on behalf of another, usually bigger, nation. Both the Americans and Soviets knew that if they were to ever face each other in an all-out war there was a good chance that it would be the end of both of their countries and quite possibly the end of all civilization on the planet. So, in order to push their political ideologies, they funded smaller governments and guerilla groups to act as their proxies.

The Korean War is considered to be the first major proxy war in the Cold War. The *Angolan Civil War* (1975–2002) was a major proxy war in Africa. In that war, the Republic of South Africa invaded Angola to support the anti-communist factions, which were also supported by the United States. Cuba sent troops to Angola to support the communist factions and the Soviet Union also sent advisors, weapons, and money to their communist allies.

The Angolan Civil War continued after the Cold War had ended.

Other notable proxy wars in the 1970s included the Rhodesian Bush War, which pitted communist rebels against the white majority government, and the Arab–Israeli Conflicts.

The 1980s saw many small proxy wars take place in Latin America. The US funded and trained the right-wing anti-communist rebels known as the *Contras*, who attempted to topple the communist *Sandinista* government in Nicaragua. The Soviet Union and Cuba in turn supported communist guerilla groups in El Salvador, Guatemala, and Bolivia, just to name a few.

Perhaps the two most important proxy wars in the Cold War were also major failures for the two major powers—Vietnam for the United States and Afghanistan for the Soviet Union.

Both of those proxy wars proved to be modern cases of David and Goliath.

VIETNAM

Vietnam is the name of a medium-sized country in Southeast Asia. If you remember, it was once part of the French colony of Indochina, but the French left when their empire started to crumble in the 1950s. Eisenhower ordered American military *"advisors"* into democratic–capitalist South Vietnam in 1955 as part of his Domino Theory policy. He believed that if South Vietnam became communist, all Southeast Asia could topple, one country after another.

President Kennedy continued Eisenhower's policy but began sending more American troops when it became clear that the South Vietnamese Army wasn't up to the task. The **North Vietnamese Army** proved to be superior in many ways and they were also supported by communist guerillas in the south, known as the **Viet Cong**.

After President Kennedy was tragically assassinated in 1963, his vice president, **Lyndon B. Johnson** (1908-1973), became president. Johnson escalated the police action into what became a full-scale war: **The Vietnam War** (1955–1975). Although the United States never officially declared war, more and more troops were sent to Vietnam after American ships were allegedly fired at, in August 1964, by North Vietnamese ships in the **Gulf of Tonkin**.

For countries in the Communist Bloc, Vietnam became the perfect proxy war. Although China and the Soviet Union were growing apart by the late 1960s (we'll talk about that a little later), they both contributed guns, anti-aircraft weapons, planes, and tanks to North Vietnam. North Vietnam and the Viet Cong couldn't have kept fighting the mighty American military without the support of China and the Soviet Union.

It is important to know that the Americans weren't the only ones fighting on the anti-communist side. Many of the non-communist governments in Asia agreed with the Americans that communism had to be stopped and therefore followed policies of **containment**. South Korea, Thailand, the Philippines, Australia, and New Zealand all sent troops to Vietnam. In fact, despite its relatively small size, Australia was America's greatest ally during the Cold War in many ways.

In the end, the Vietnam War proved to be a major victory for the Communist Bloc in the Cold War. More than 50,000 Americans died in a war that deeply divided the American population. It became too costly for the Americans and their allies to continue what was essentially a *"war of occupation,"* so in 1975 the last American troops left South Vietnam. Communist forces were not only able to take South Vietnam, they also took over the neighboring countries of **Cambodia** and **Laos,** which also became communist.

The Soviet Union was probably the biggest winner in Vietnam, but would their good fortune last?

CHINA GOES NUCLEAR

Mao Zedong was a true believer in communism. He wanted to transform his somewhat backward and rural country into a peasant's paradise, and he also wanted to push communism outside of his country at whatever cost. During the Korean War, Mao demonstrated to the world that China was willing to fight on behalf of its communist allies, but the war exposed China as a technologically backward country. Most of the Chinese soldiers were under-equipped and many didn't even have guns.

So, Mao decided that the best way to even the odds with the Americans was to build nuclear weapons.

China began its nuclear weapons program in the late 1950s and at first was almost entirely dependent on the Soviets. The Soviets built most of the missiles and the infrastructure that would be needed to use them. However, as cooperation between the two communist nations progressed, problems between them started to come to the surface.

Mao and the Communist Party of China believed that they were the true followers of communism and that the Soviet Union had grown *"decadent"* and turned their backs on socialist beliefs. The Chinese disagreed with how the Soviets basically erased the memory of Joseph Stalin from their country and worse, how Khrushchev made overtures to the West with talk of *"peaceful coexistence."*

As you know from this book, Khrushchev was still very much a communist and supported communist governments and movements around the world, but to Mao that just wasn't enough. To him, true communism needed to be more confrontational against the West. Mao decided that China could finish making its first nuclear bomb without the Soviets.

On October 16, 1964, the Chinese tested their first nuclear bomb at an underground testing site. China had officially joined the nuclear club along with the USA, USSR, UK, and France. Although it never had anywhere near the number of nuclear weapons that the Soviets or Americans had, just having a few, combined with their massive army, was enough to prevent any attacks on Chinese soil.

The rift between China and the Soviet Union continued until they formally split in 1966 in what became known as the **Sino–Soviet Split**. *"Sino"* is another word for Chinese. The USSR and China competed for influence among the smaller Communist/Eastern Bloc countries from that point forward and generally approached relations with the US and the West quite differently.

THE PRAGUE SPRING

During the late 1960s there were a lot of changes happening in Western countries. Students were protesting the Vietnam War, among other things, and forcing their leaders to listen. By 1968, some of that spirit of protest had made it through the Iron Curtain. Alexander Dubček became the leader of Czechoslovakia in January 1968 and immediately stated that he would embark on a series of reforms.

Leonid Brezhnev, the man who replaced Khrushchev as leader of the Soviet Union, didn't like what he was hearing. It was beginning to sound a lot like what had happened years earlier in Hungary, so he called Dubček in for a meeting.

But before the meeting took place in March, students began protesting on the streets of Czechoslovakia's capital city, Prague, as well as other major cities in the country. They demanded more political rights, less press censorship, and the right to travel within and away from their country more freely. Dubček indicated that he was willing to listen to the youth and allow more *"democratization."*

Brezhnev and the other Eastern Bloc leaders didn't want to hear the word democratization. So, on the night of August 20–21, more than 200,000 Warsaw Pact troops and over 2,000 tanks entered Czechoslovakia, arrested Dubček, and put the country under martial law. Dubček was brought to Moscow, where he was intimidated until he promised to end his campaign of reforms. He was removed from his position in April 1969 and lived a quiet existence until he died in a car accident in 1992.

Unlike the Hungarian Revolution, there wasn't much bloodshed during the Prague Spring. Around 100 protesters did die fighting the Soviets, but Dubček publicly told his people not to resist, which no doubt cut down on the number of casualties.

The U.S. and most of the other Western nations said little about the events, as they had given up on Eastern Europe in the 1950s. The Prague Spring's most important Cold War consequences were the divisions it caused within the communist world. The Chinese believed that they were possibly the next victims of Soviet aggression, so they built up their forces along their border with the Soviet Union. The troop buildup led to a series of border clashes in 1969, which further hurt Chinese–Soviet relations.

The small communist nation of Albania was upset with the Soviet Union's actions, so they moved further from them and closer to China politically. Finally, many communists in Western countries also disagreed with the Soviet Union's actions in Czechoslovakia. Less support for the Soviet Union in Western nations made it harder for the KGB to find sympathetic agents for their spy networks.

DÉTENTE?

The 1970s was the Brezhnev Era in the Soviet Union, and it was also the period in the Cold War known as the *Détente*. So, what does this word mean and why was it important in the Cold War? Well, détente is a French word that means *"relaxing"* or *"cooling off,"* which in our case relates to the relaxing of relations between the USSR and USA. The people of the Soviet Union and the United States were tired of being on edge for most of the 1960s and their leaders knew it. Brezhnev's policy of forming better relations with the US was generally received well by the Russian people as well as the leaders of the Communist Party.

Likewise, in the United States, the Détente was viewed positively by members of both the Democratic and Republican parties. Richard Nixon (1913–1994), who was a leading anti-communist in the 1950s when he was Eisenhower's vice president, was elected president in 1968, partially on a platform of Détente. Nixon's two immediate successors, Republican Gerald Ford (1913–2006) and Democrat Jimmy Carter (1924–), also carried out the policy of Détente.

Détente was often carried out in the form of treaties that limited the number and type of weapons used by the major powers.

In 1972, Nixon and Brezhnev formalized the *Strategic Arms Limitation Talks Agreement (SALT)*, which was followed by SALT II in 1979: both treaties limited the number of nuclear missiles both countries could have. When SALT I was signed, the Biological Weapons Convention, which prevented the further development of biological weapons by signatory nations, and the Anti-Ballistic Missile Treaty (ABM) were also signed.

Some of the treaties signed by the USA and USSR had more to do with fostering the spirit of goodwill rather than reducing weapons. For instance, the Helsinki Accords was a 1975 non-binding act signed by the United States, Canada, and most of the European nations that sought to respect human rights while defusing Cold War tensions.

The era of cooperation that the Détente brought even went into outer space!

The *Apollo-Soyuz Test Project (ASTP)* of 1975 was the first cooperative American–Soviet space flight. It had a major impact on the cultural landscape of the United States during the 1970s, as millions of Americans witnessed their astronauts shake hands and exchange gifts and flags with the Soviet cosmonauts.

The 1970s was truly an era of optimism and hope for better relations between East and West. But would it last?

NIXON IN CHINA

One of the biggest events to take place during the Détente was President Nixon visiting the People's Republic of China (Communist China) from February 21 to 28, 1972. Today it may not seem like that big of a deal, since China allows its people to leave and allows foreigners to visit, but in the middle of the Cold War it was a major event. China had been closed to the Western world since it became communist. Mao Zedong remained a true communist, but he was a smart man who understood that China had more problems than the East–West conflict.

Remember that China and the Soviet Union were having problems by the late 1960s and even had some border skirmishes in 1968. Mao wanted to exploit that division by moving his country a little closer to the West.

For his part, Nixon also viewed his visit to China as a situation where he could gain leverage on the Soviet Union. Nixon reasoned that if the Soviets thought the Chinese were becoming friendlier with the Americans, then he could get more out of the USSR in future negotiations.

Make no mistake, the Cold War was still happening, it had just become more about political negotiations and gaining leverage in the 1970s.

Nixon and Mao met one time during the visit, agreeing to many important issues. The Chinese agreed to stop threatening Taiwan and the Americans, in turn, agreed to recognize Communist China as *"the"* legitimate Chinese government. Both countries also agreed to open trade.

But for animal lovers, the most important development of Nixon's visit to China was when Mao gave a pair of giant pandas—Hsing-Hsing (male) and Ling-Ling (female)—to the National Zoo in Washington, D.C. The extremely cute pandas quickly became the most popular attraction in the zoo! Although an endangered species and China's national animal, more giant pandas were shipped to American zoos in the following decades in what became known as *panda diplomacy*.

You see, not everything that happened during the Cold War was bad.

NOT SO FAST!

There may have been a Détente in the Cold War during the 1970s, but that didn't mean that the major players weren't trying to expand their influence through their proxies. The 1970s saw a new front open in the Cold War—Latin America. The United States had a deep interest in stopping the spread of communism in Central and South America at the very beginning of the Cold War, as it considered that region to be its *"backyard."* Eisenhower sponsored a right-wing military coup in *Guatemala* to overthrow its left-wing government, and we have discussed how much of a problem Castro and Cuba were for Kennedy.

In the 1970s, the Cubans and Soviets began funding left-wing guerilla organizations throughout South America, so the Americans responded by supporting right-wing military dictatorships in Argentina, Brazil, Paraguay, Uruguay, and Bolivia. Collectively these countries, along with Chile, are known as the *Southern Cone* because they are the southernmost countries in South America.

For President Nixon, though, Chile was a problem in the region.

The Chilean people democratically elected an open socialist named Salvador Allende to be their president in 1970. At first it didn't seem like much of a problem. Socialists had been elected to power throughout the world, including in Europe, and this hadn't caused problems for the United States. But Allende began making overtures to Cuba and the Soviet Union and when he *nationalized* many American companies, it led to a crisis in the US. American corporations wanted Allende gone, as did many political conservatives, who viewed him as only half a step from being a full-fledged communist.

Nixon basically looked at the election of Allende and said to the Chilean people, *"Not so fast!"*

So, the United States supported a military coup led by General *Augusto Pinochet* in 1973. Allende killed himself, because he knew that he would probably be tortured and then executed if captured by the military. Chile then fell in line with the other countries of the Southern Cone.

The next step for the right-wing governments of the Southern Cone was to form an alliance and then an aggressive anti-communist campaign called *Operation Condor* in 1975. Operation Condor involved the militaries of those countries carrying out assassinations, kidnappings, and military operations against real and suspected communists in their countries. The United States provided major funding and training for Operation Condor until it finally ended in 1989.

SECOND QUIZ TIME!

1. What was the Latin American country where the nuclear missile crisis in 1962 took place?

2. What was the word for *"astronaut"* in the Soviet Union?

3. Name one of the USA's allies that also fought in the Vietnam War.

4. _____ was the capital of Czechoslovakia and the scene of anti-Soviet protests in 1968.

5. Who was the bald leader of the Soviet Union after Joseph Stalin?

6. What year did American President Richard Nixon visit China?

7. Who was the American president during the Berlin Crisis of 1961?

INTERESTING QUOTES

Politicians are the same all over.
They promise to build a bridge even where there is no river.
Nikita Khrushchev

As we express our gratitude, we must never forget that
the highest appreciation is not to utter words, but to live by them.

John F. Kennedy

Children are the masters of the new society.
Mao Zedong

LIFE IN THE WEST DURING THE COLD WAR

We've covered how there was a fair amount of fear and paranoia in America during the Cold War, especially in the 1950s and '60s. Many people thought that communists were either going to take over the government from within or rain missiles down on the country from Russia.

But there was another side of life in the West during the Cold War.

Most of the 1950s and '60s were times of great economic prosperity in the United States, as well as for many of its allies. The 1957 Chevy became a symbol of American ambition and success and suburbs and subdivisions were continually built well into the 1980s. The 1950s and '60s were also a time of great social change in the West.

The *Civil Rights* movement took place, which led to the end of legalized racial segregation and discrimination. Laws were changed that made it possible for many black Americans to vote for the first time and to live in neighborhoods that were once considered off-limits.

There was also a great generational change in the West during the Cold War. As mentioned earlier, when World War II veterans returned home, one of the first things they did was to start families. The result was the *Baby Boom Generation* in the United States and Western Europe. The Baby Boomers grew up with what was at the time the new sounds of *Rock 'n' Roll*, which often confused and upset their parents. By the time the Baby Boomers started to reach young adulthood and college age in the late 1960s, the men found themselves facing the prospect of being drafted to fight in Vietnam. Most who were drafted did their duty and went, but some actively protested the war.

Youth opposition to the Vietnam War took place throughout the West and was part of a much wider movement known as the *Counterculture Movement*. It was called that because it was against, or counter to, many of the old, conservative beliefs of the previous generations.

The protests caused a lot of tensions and set people against each other. However, by the 1970s the chaos had for the most part subsided. In the United States in particular, most people wanted to get back to work and focus on their families. As the Détente between the Soviet Union and the United States took place, Americans celebrated the *Bicentennial* (200-year anniversary) of their country in 1976.

A major scandal known as *Watergate* was taking place in the White House and President Nixon resigned because of it, but most Americans felt safe and confident that better days were still ahead.

MOBILE MISSILES AND SUBMARINES

The United States took an early and wide lead in the nuclear arms race, but by the 1970s the Soviet Union had reached *parity*. Parity in this case meant that the Soviet Union had around the same number of nuclear weapons as the United States. So how were the Soviets able to do this?

The USSR had an economic and technological disadvantage compared to the USA, so they had to be a bit creative. In 1959, the Soviets began by creating an entire branch of their military that was dedicated to creating and deploying nuclear missiles—the *Strategic Missile Forces (SMS)*. They built and maintained the silos for the Soviet Union's *intercontinental ballistic missiles (ICBMs)*, but even then, the USSR lagged behind the USA's arsenal in terms of efficiency.

So, by the 1980s the Soviets came up with a couple of unique solutions. One of the solutions to their problem was the *Topol* rocket. The Topol is an ICBM that is launched from a large vehicle with the capability of hitting targets throughout the Western world. The mobile missiles proved to be much more cost efficient than permanent missile silos and their mobility gave the Soviets another advantage because they were extremely difficult for the Americans to track.

In the early 1960s, both sides began arming submarines with nuclear missiles, although once again the US took the early lead. Since the Soviets had far fewer military bases around the world than the Americans, they developed bigger submarines with better missiles. By the early 1980s, the Soviets had developed the *Typhoon* class of submarines, which were the largest submarines ever built. Typhoon class submarines were massive, at more than 500 feet long, and armed with twenty nuclear missiles that could create widespread destruction very quickly.

Although the Soviets were in danger of falling behind the Americans in the arms race, the combination of mobile missiles and submarines helped them maintain parity.

THE ARAB–ISRAELI CONFLICTS

In 1948, the Jewish state of Israel was formed from what was once the British possession of Palestine. Many in the West believed that it was a good idea since there were already many Jews living in Palestine and millions more were displaced due to World War II.

But not everyone was happy. As soon as the state of Israel was announced, many of the Arab nations attacked Israel, setting off the *Arab–Israeli War* (1948–1949). The state of Israel survived the war, but it would just be the first in several conflicts that are known collectively as the *Arab–Israeli* conflict. The larger Arab states in the region, such as Egypt and Syria, viewed Israel as an enemy for nationalistic and religious reasons. They believed that the Israelis had treated the non-Jewish Palestinians unfairly, kicking many of them out of their homes. The major Arab nations were also Muslim, while Israel was a Jewish country.

It didn't take long for the Arab–Israeli Conflicts to become another setting in the Cold War. When Egyptian Army colonel *Gamal Nasser* (1918–1970) became his country's leader through a 1954 coup, he developed close ties to the Soviet Union. The Egyptians received military and financial aid from the Soviet Union and set the tone among other Arab nations that the Soviet Union was their friend. Hafez al-Assad, the leader of Syria, followed Nasser's lead by becoming friends with the Soviets. On the other side, the US favored Israel with plenty of military aid.

As the Middle Eastern countries built up their militaries, small-scale wars regularly broke out from the 1950s through the 1970s. In 1956, France, the UK, and Israel attacked Egypt over control of the *Suez Canal*. Although the three countries won the initial battle, they were forced to withdraw due to international pressure, which ended up being a moral victory for the Egyptians.

The Israelis struck the Arab forces again on June 5, 1967, destroying most of the air forces of Egypt, Syria, Iraq, and Jordan in what became known as the *Six Day War*. Israel massively extended its territory as a result of this war.

On October 6, 1973, Egypt and Syria returned the favor by conducting their own first strike against Israel in what is known as the *Yom Kippur War*. Although the Arab forces had the early advantage, the Israelis regrouped. Once the Israelis started getting the better of the Arabs, the USSR threatened to intervene, which brought the US to the table to help arrange a ceasefire on October 25.

Egypt eventually moved away from Soviet influence and even signed a peace agreement with Israel in 1978 known as the *Camp David Accords*.

DID YOU KNOW?

- The People's Republic of North Korea (Communist North Korea) is ruled by a dynasty. Kim Il-Sung (1912–1994) was the first premier and later the first president of North Korea. His son, Kim Jong-Il (1942–2011) succeeded him and after he died his son, Kim Jong-Un (1984–) came to power.

- The term *nuclear triad* refers to countries that have the following nuclear weapons capabilities: intercontinental ballistic missiles (ICBMs), submarine launched ballistic missiles (SLBMs), and strategic air bombers.

- The Camp David Accords were signed by Egyptian President Anwar Sadat (1918–1981) and Israeli Prime Minister Menachem Begin (1913–1992). American President Jimmy Carter served as the mediator of the talks at the presidential retreat of Camp David in Maryland.

- The buildup of nuclear arsenals on both sides during the Cold War became known as *mutual assured destruction (MAD)*. The idea was that neither side would strike first because it meant that both countries would be wiped out in the process.

- Because giant pandas are an endangered species, the Chinese were reluctant to give any of the cute animals to other countries. They worked out a loan program with American zoos to house the animals on a long-term basis. Today, giant pandas can be seen in zoos in Memphis, Atlanta, and Washington.

- Operation Condor was named for the Andean condor, which is a large vulture native to many countries in South America.

- During Operation Condor, many of the right-wing governments relied on *paramilitaries* to carry out their operations. Paramilitary groups were non-government organizations that were anti-communist. By having the paramilitary groups do their dirty work, the governments of Operation Condor could deny they were directly involved with political violence.

- Anwar Sadat was assassinated by Egyptian members of the *Muslim Brotherhood* for signing the Camp David Accords.

IRAN THROWS A TWIST INTO THE COLD WAR

In January 1979, protests began in Iran that would affect the course of the Cold War and are still being felt today. You see, for many reasons Iran was a bit of a wild card. Although Iran is a predominantly Muslim nation, most of the people follow the branch of Islam known as **Shia**, which in most other countries is followed by the minority of Muslims. Also, unlike many of the Muslims of the Middle East who are Arabs or Arabic speaking, Iranians are ethnically **Persians** and speak the Persian or Farsi language. You might be surprised to know that the Farsi language is more like European languages than it is Arabic. Finally, Iran's location in central Asia also meant that it has had connections with Russia (later the Soviet Union) for several centuries.

But in modern times the government of Iran moved closer to the United States. Iran was ruled by a monarchy in the 20th century. In particular, a family known as the **Pahlavi Dynasty** that had ruled the country since 1925. In 1978, a man named **Mohammad Reza Pahlavi** (1919–1980) ruled the country as its **shah** or king. Reza formed close ties to the United States, but he was a brutal leader and very unpopular with his people. As the protests against his rule grew, Islamic fundamentalists organized and became the leaders of the protest movement.

Violence broke out and in January 1979 the Pahlavi family left Iran for good.

A religious leader named Ruhollah Khomeini (1902–1989) came to power as Iran's Supreme Leader. This meant that Iran officially became a **theocracy** or a religious government, which had many implications in the Cold War.

The Soviet Union was the first country to recognize the **Islamic Republic of Iran**, but Khomeini was not too fond of communism or the Soviets. Since atheism is a central belief of communism, Khomeini was immediately hostile to the USSR, calling it the *"little Satan."* The *"great Satan,"* though, was the United States.

Khomeini personally hated the US for supporting the Pahlavi family, and was also opposed to what he saw as decadent American values. He routinely gave anti-American speeches, riling up large crowds of his followers. Finally, in November 1979, a large group of militant students took over the American embassy in the capital of Tehran. The Americans were held as hostages for 444 days, before they were released on January 20, 1981.

Both the USSR and USA would actually support Iran's enemy, Iraq, in the Iran–Iraq War, proving that lines were often blurred during the Cold War.

THE MIRACLE ON ICE

During the Cold War, the Olympics were about showing which bloc had the best athletes. Usually, the Soviet Union and America were the top two nations, and in the Winter Olympics the Soviets seemed to dominate. When the 1980 Winter Olympics began in Lake Placid, New York, things were a little different. It was clear that the Détente of the 1970s was over and the Cold War was heating up again.

The Soviet Union had just invaded the central Asian country of Afghanistan on December 24, 1979. In addition to the Soviet invasion of Afghanistan, the United States was experiencing an economic recession: unemployment, interest rates, and inflation were all high.

Many Americans were looking for something to believe in and it came with the USA men's hockey team.

The experts didn't give Team USA much of a chance. The Soviet team was the hands-down favorite to win the gold medal, as the team was made up of the best players in the Soviet Union. On the other hand, the US team was primarily made up of college players, and none of them were professionals. Some would later play professional hockey, but many did not. American coach **Herb Brooks** knew that he was in for the biggest test of his life. Almost all the American players were from either Minnesota or New England, but there was something quite American about all of them. Although outside of the Upper Midwest and New England few people played hockey, the American people quickly identified with the scrappy young men from Minnesota and Massachusetts.

Brooks knew that the Soviets had more raw talent than his team, but he got the Americans to play as a team and to bring their hard-nosed style of North American hockey right to the Soviets! The two teams advanced through the group stages of the competition, so when they met on February 22 the stage was set for an epic showdown.

The game was rough and tough and although the Soviets scored first, the Americans quickly responded. With the Soviets up 3–2 going into the third and final period, it looked like the game was theirs. But the Americans scored two goals in the third—one by Mike Johnson and another one by USA captain Mike Eruzione to put the Americans up 4–3. The Soviets were stunned and had clearly underestimated the young Americans.

As the clock ran out on the game, American broadcaster Al Michaels famously said, *"Do you believe in miracles? YES!"*

The victory is still seen as one of the greatest upsets in sports history and a brief moment when all Americans united behind a group of unlikely heroes.

THE SOVIET UNION'S VIETNAM

As mentioned in the last section, the Soviet Union invaded Afghanistan on December 24, 1979. Afghani communists had taken over the government of that country in 1978, but fundamentalist Muslims resisted their ideas, leading to a civil war. The Soviets invaded to help stabilize the communist government, but instead they found themselves in a long, drawn-out war that they couldn't win. It was much like Vietnam had been for the United States. The *Soviet–Afghan War* (1979–1989) is often remembered as the USSR's Vietnam.

The Soviet invasion of Afghanistan immediately set off an important chain of events throughout the world. The United States, Argentina, China, Japan, West Germany, and several other countries *boycotted* the 1980 Summer Olympics in Moscow, USSR. A boycott is when a person or group refuses to participate in something based on principle.

Brezhnev argued that the USSR was totally justified in its invasion of Afghanistan, because the communist government was their ally and Russia had a long history of friendly relations with Afghanistan. Afghanistan is fairly close to Russia/USSR so many world leaders were willing to look away. But in 1981 the United States had a new president, who was much more like Eisenhower in his approach to communism.

When *Ronald Reagan* (1911–2004) was elected president in 1980, he promised to challenge communism throughout the world, so he looked at Afghanistan as one of his first tests. Reagan and the Congress authorized the US military and the CIA to give weapons, training, and intelligence to anti-Soviet, Sunni Muslim fighters, known as the *Mujahideen*. The Mujahideen used hit and run and other guerilla tactics against the much better armed and trained Soviet Army. To make matters more complicated, Iran was also training and funding anti-Soviet Shia Muslim guerillas, who would also fight the Sunni Mujahideen from time to time.

The Soviets found themselves in an impossible situation. They would take ground and establish bases, only to be attacked later by Mujahideen snipers and bombers. The Soviets never knew who their friends or foes were, just like the Americans in Vietnam.

The proxy war in Afghanistan dragged on and on, until nearly 15,000 Soviet soldiers were killed in the war. The war became too costly and caused a serious drain on the Soviet system, which was already experiencing serious economic problems by the mid-1980s. The war also became unpopular with the people of the USSR and, although they didn't protest it the way Americans did during Vietnam, it led many to question the abilities of the Soviet system.

THE IRON LADY

When Ronald Reagan became president, leaders and the media from many different countries portrayed him as a cowboy and made fun of his acting background. Many leaders weren't very willing to get on board with Reagan's aggressive anti-communist policies, but the leader of one important country was more than willing to join him. *Margaret Thatcher* (1925–2013) became the Prime Minister of the United Kingdom as the leader of the majority Conservative Party. She led her nation's government for the entire 1980s and was perhaps Reagan's closest ally. She may have appeared as a prim and proper British lady, but she was known for being tough, which is how she earned the nickname *"The Iron Lady."*

Thatcher was born Margaret Hilda Roberts, to a middle-class English family. She showed great aptitude in school and went to college, where she met her future husband David. Thatcher was a true trailblazer. She became a lawyer in the early 1950s when few women were and later joined the Conservative Party. She steadily worked her way up the ranks until she became the UK's first female prime minister.

Before becoming prime minister, Thatcher had already acquired a reputation for being a tough lady and an ardent anti-communist. A Soviet reporter called her the *"Iron Lady"* in 1976 as an insult, but she took it as a compliment and the name stuck. After all, a woman had to be tough to be in politics back then!

In a time when many Western European countries were questioning if they should stay in NATO, Thatcher increased Britain's role in the alliance in terms of troops and funding. She also made sure that Britain's military was modernized, including its small but formidable nuclear weapons arsenal. Thatcher also authorized support for the anti-communist Mujahideen in Afghanistan.

Like Reagan, Thatcher was routinely criticized and even made fun of by the press, but true to her nickname she usually gave no reaction. The Iron Lady was truly one of the most important figures of the late Cold War.

AN EVIL EMPIRE?

On March 8, 1983, President Reagan gave a speech to a group of Evangelical Christians in Florida where he described the Soviet Union as an *"evil empire."* At the time, the speech really wasn't that controversial. Most people knew that Reagan was very anti-communist and most Americans agreed with his sentiment to some degree. The speech was also given at a time that was between some major Cold War events.

Yuri Andropov (1914–1984) became the leader of the Soviet Union on November 12, 1982. He was no reformer and was more than happy to continue the Cold War with Reagan. Then, in October 1983, just months after Reagan's speech, the United States invaded the tiny Caribbean nation of *Grenada*. A communist government had come to power in Grenada in 1979 and Reagan wanted it gone, so he sent the Marines down there to quickly take care of it. Then, on September 1, 1983, the Soviets shot down *Korean Air Lines Flight 007*, killing all 269 people on board, including American Congressman Larry McDonald. It turns out that the flight had veered into Soviet airspace and the Soviets shot it down, thinking it was either a spy plane or that they were under attack.

By the end of 1983 it seemed to most Americans that the USSR was an evil empire, but was it really?

The truth is that communism was certainly a flawed system and there were countless human rights abuses under communist dictatorships, but most people in the Soviet Union weren't members of the Communist Party.

Censorship heavily controlled what people could say and there were few consumer options. Waiting in long lines to buy bread and other food items was quite common and it was a luxury for a family to own one car, or a refrigerator, or even a television set. Single family homes were also quite rare, with most families living in large apartment blocks where multiple families shared a single kitchen.

Still, even with those inconveniences, the people of the Soviet Union enjoyed many of the same pastimes as Americans. The Black Sea region was a popular vacation destination and by the 1960s, Western music and clothing styles were becoming popular with the youth, although they were usually considered illegal.

And like the United States, the Soviet Union was quite diverse. If you remember, Russia was only the largest republic within the Soviet Union. Moscow was quite an international city during the Cold War, where you could meet people from all over the USSR, as well as other communist nations, on any day.

Also, like Americans, the average Soviet citizen was quite scared of the possibility of World War III and nuclear annihilation.

SOLIDARITY

Few countries suffered more, during and just after World War II, than Poland. The Nazis and Soviets first split the country in two and then took turns occupying it over the course of the war. After the war, the Soviets imposed a puppet communist government on the Polish people. The fact is that the Polish people were never onboard with communism and historically were closer to Western Europe than Russia or the Soviet Union. Although the Polish people are Slavic like the Russians, they are also ardent Roman Catholics and have historically had deeper ties with Germany, Austria, and Hungary than with Russia.

But the Polish people dealt with the situation the best they could.

They lived their lives just as most of the people behind the Iron Curtain did, but economic problems in Poland in the late 1970s brought resentment with the system to the surface. Workers in the docks of the port city of Gdansk began protesting their stagnant wages and treatment by the government. Then, on August 31, 1980, *Lech Wałęsa* and some other dock workers formed the **Independent Self-governing Trade Union *"Solidarity,"*** which became known worldwide as the *Solidarity Movement*.

Trade unions weren't illegal in the Eastern Bloc. In fact, because communism claimed to be a political system for the workers, unions were even promoted by communist governments. But only certain unions were promoted. The Solidarity Movement was the first independent union to form in a communist country and it very quickly became a problem for both the Polish Communist Party and the Soviet Union.

By the middle of 1981 there were ten million members of Solidarity, as it formed a broad coalition of members from different backgrounds. Ronald Reagan was an open supporter of Solidarity and authorized the CIA to help the movement behind the scenes. The Catholic Church, with its Polish born pope (we'll get to him in a minute), was also a vocal supporter of the Solidarity Movement.

The Solidarity Movement avoided violent clashes with the Polish government, which helped it gain sympathy and support around the world. Today, many historians see the Solidarity Movement as an important part of the Cold War and the beginning of the end for communist rule in Eastern Europe.

THE ANTI-COMMUNIST POPE

Pope John Paul II (1920–2005) was one of the most important figures of the late Cold War. He was born Karol Józef Wojtyła in Poland, to a Polish father and a Lithuanian mother, during a period in history that was known for violence and political instability. He lived through the Nazi occupation of Poland and the first few years of communism, before he decided to dedicate his life to God and the Catholic Church.

He served as a priest for several years in his native country and because the Communist Party's official stance on religion was atheism, he often had to hide his missionary activities from the government. Karol later joined the church hierarchy and due to his efforts behind the Iron Curtain, along with his intelligence and education, he was elected Pope of the Roman Catholic Church in 1978.

He traveled the world extensively, met with leaders from several countries, and was not afraid to condemn communism, believing it was a godless faith. Although he was often vocal against some of the right-wing dictatorships in Latin America, he was equally opposed to the communist guerillas who opposed them.

Pope John Paul II became a problem for the Polish communists, who tried to ruin his reputation by making up many lies. It was clear that the pope was changing people's hearts in both the West and East, demonstrating that people could live together, when his life almost came to an end.

A Turkish nationalist shot Pope John Paul II during a procession in Vatican City on May 13, 1981. The pope was shot in the stomach, but miraculously survived and made a full recovery.

After his recovery from the attempted assassination, Pope John Paul II became one of the leading supporters of the Solidary Movement in the early to mid-1980s and developed a close relationship with Ronald Reagan. He continued to speak out for the remainder of his life against what he believed were social injustices.

During the 1980s, Pope John Paul II believed that communism was one of the biggest injustices in world history and he certainly played a major role in its eventual collapse in Europe.

SAVING OR ENDING COMMUNISM?

When **Mikhail Gorbachev** (1931–) became the leader of the Soviet Union, it was clear to many that he was a little different than the previous leaders. He dressed nice, made a habit of talking to citizens on the streets, and openly talked about ending the Cold War. *"Gorby,"* as Gorbachev became affectionately known, met with Reagan to discuss both countries reducing their nuclear arsenals, and he began mending fences with other countries as well. All of this was part of Gorbachev's plans known as **Perestroika** and **Glasnost**.

Perestroika, which in English roughly translates to *"restructuring,"* was an attempt to end corruption in the Soviet bureaucracy and to introduce some elements of the free market to the economy. Restrictions on imports were eased and the first McDonald's was built in the Soviet Union!

Glasnost, which translates to *"openness,"* was much more widespread and involved a complete dismantling of the traditional police state in the Soviet Union. Under Glasnost, citizens were given more freedom, Moscow began to ease its control over the non-Russian Soviet republics and Warsaw Pact nations, Soviet citizens could leave the country more, and Westerners were allowed to visit the Soviet Union.

Gorbachev's plan was to save the communist system by making it more efficient and less corrupt. He also wanted to make it seem more appealing and less scary to the West.

But the reality is that Glasnost and Perestroika led to the end of the Soviet Union and communism in Eastern Europe. First the Warsaw Pact countries began peacefully overthrowing their communist governments in 1989. Then the various republics of the Soviet Union began leaving the USSR in 1990.

Once the people of Russia and the Soviet Union began getting a little taste of freedom, money, and cheeseburgers, they wanted to have it all the time. The Cold War was about to be over, but it wasn't the American military that won it, it was the American dollar and McDonald's that earned the victory!

"TEAR DOWN THIS WALL"

Reagan and the other leaders in the West knew that when Gorbachev came to power, change was in the air. They also knew that the Western economy was going to win the Cold War. Besides the Western consumer goods that began flooding into the Soviet Union, the American economy was just too big for the Soviet economy. The Americans were able to simply outspend the Soviets, in military and scientific research.

So, when Reagan visited Berlin on June 12, 1987, he made a historic speech in front of the **Brandenburg Gate**. The site was chosen because it was directly in front of the Berlin Wall. The speech was basically a call for Gorbachev to allow Germany to reunify. Part of it read:

"General Secretary Gorbachev, if you seek peace, if you seek prosperity for the Soviet Union and Eastern Europe, if you seek liberalization, come here to this gate. Mr. Gorbachev, open this gate! Mr. Gorbachev, tear down this wall!"

The speech wasn't covered very much by the press and it didn't seem to have much of an effect on Gorbachev, but just over two years later, on November 9, 1989, the German people themselves dismantled the Berlin Wall. Germany became a unified country once again in 1990.

As we talked about in the previous chapter, the Warsaw Pact countries quickly dropped their communist governments and the Soviet republics followed. But not everything went so smoothly.

Violence broke out in the central Asian Soviet republic of **Azerbaijan** throughout 1990 as it moved toward independence from the Soviet Union, and Gorbachev himself became the victim of an attempted coup.

Hardline members of the Communist Party had had enough of Gorbachev's reforms, so on August 19, 1991, they decided to use the military and KGB to take the government back. Future Russian president Boris Yeltsin turned out with thousands of citizens to oppose the hardliners peacefully. Although three protesters were killed, the coup failed.

Once the coup was suppressed, the breakup of the Soviet Union continued. On Christmas Day, 1991, Gorbachev announced to his people that he would no longer be the leader of the Soviet Union; the Soviet flag was lowered from the **Kremlin** and replaced with the current Russian flag.

On December 26, 1991, the USSR was officially dissolved, and the Cold War had ended.

THIRD QUIZ TIME!

1. Who was the UK/Britain's prime minister during most of the 1980s?

   a. Evita Peron
   b. Margaret Thatcher
   c. Bill Murray

2. This country became the Soviet Union's *"Vietnam."*

   a. Afghanistan
   b. South Africa
   c. Belize

3. The _____ were a major part of the Cold War in the 1970s.

   a. The Arab–Israeli Conflicts
   b. Mexican Conflicts
   c. The Australian Conflicts

4. What was the private Polish trade union anti-communist movement of the 1980s called?

   a. Unity
   b. Hard Work
   c. Solidarity

5. _____ was a Polish pope who was opposed to communism.

   a. Billy Joe Bob
   b. John Paul II
   c. Juan Garcia

INTERESTING QUOTES

I do not know anyone who has gotten to the top without hard work. That is the recipe. It will not always get you to the top, but it will get you pretty near.

Margaret Thatcher

Freedom consists not in doing what we like, but in having the right to do what we ought.

Pope John Paul II

If you are not moving forward, you are moving backward.

Mikhail Gorbachev

QUIZ ANSWERS

Answers: First Quiz Time!

1. a. USSR/Soviet Union
2. c. UK/Great Britain
3. a. Iron Curtain
4. b. A military alliance of European communist countries
5. b. The Korean War

Answers: Second Quiz Time!

1. Cuba
2. Cosmonaut
3. South Vietnam, Thailand, South Korea, Australia, New Zealand, the Philippines
4. Prague
5. Nikita Khrushchev
6. 1972
7. John F. Kennedy

Answers: Third Quiz Time!

1. b. Margaret Thatcher
2. a. Afghanistan
3. a. The Arab–Israeli Conflicts
4. c. Solidarity
5. b. John Paul II

CONCLUSION

There is little doubt that the Cold War was one of the most important periods in world history. It was a showdown between two great nations and political ideologies, where one wrong move by either side could have thrust the entire globe into World War III. Although the Cold War officially ended in 1991, with the breakup of the Soviet Union, its effects can still be felt throughout the world.

Cuba remains a communist dictatorship and though it has opened somewhat to the outside world, the government is still politically repressive. Cuba and the United States still have not **normalized** relations.

China is also an interesting post-Cold War story. The Communist Party still runs the Chinese government, but it now allows a certain amount of capitalism and free trade. The Chinese government also allows outsiders to visit and even invites foreign professionals to work and live there in order to teach its people new skills. Chinese citizens are also allowed to leave their country for vacations, school, and even permanently for jobs.

Finally, there is Russia. Russia experienced quite a few economic and social problems during the 1990s. Organized crime became a noticeably big problem in Russia's biggest cities, Chechnyan terrorists attacked Moscow multiple times, unemployment was high, and corruption threatened to derail the democratic process. By the 2000s, though, under the leadership of Vladimir Putin, Russia overcame many of those problems and has since reasserted itself as a world leader.

In fact, in many ways some things haven't changed.

In recent years, many American politicians have blamed Putin, and Russians in general, for election losses, claiming *"Russian interference"* without any solid evidence. The accusations have angered many in Russia and have led to the worst Russian–American relations since the Cold War. Many people are reminded that the recent anti-Russian sentiment by some American politicians sounds very paranoid and reminiscent of the Red Scare.

Whatever is the case, the reality is that Russia today, just like the USSR during the Cold War, is a major military, economic, and diplomatic power that can't be ignored. The Cold War may be over, and the Russian bear may have been defeated, but he is still around.

Made in the USA
Las Vegas, NV
25 October 2020

10330781R00057